Burns and Oates

Drops of oil from the lamp of the sanctuary

Or, Unction of the Seven Sacraments

Burns and Oates

Drops of oil from the lamp of the sanctuary
Or, Unction of the Seven Sacraments

ISBN/EAN: 9783742865090

Manufactured in Europe, USA, Canada, Australia, Japa

Cover: Foto ©Lupo / pixelio.de

Manufactured and distributed by brebook publishing software
(www.brebook.com)

Burns and Oates

Drops of oil from the lamp of the sanctuary

" And God said, Be light made.
And light was made."

Laus Deo Semper.

"Thou shalt make also seven lamps, and shalt set them upon the candlestick, to give light over-against."

—*Exodus* xxv. 37.

"Command the children of Israel that they bring thee the purest oil of the olives, and beaten with a pestle : that a lamp may burn always, in the tabernacle of the testimony, without the veil that hangs before the testimony. And Aaron and his sons shall order it, that it may give light before the Lord until the morning. It shall be a perpetual observance throughout their successions among the children of Israel." —*Exodus* xxvii. 20, 21.

Drops of Oil

from the

Lamp of the Sanctuary;

OR,

UNCTION OF THE SEVEN SACRAMENTS.

London:

BURNS & OATES,

17 & 18 PORTMAN STREET AND 63 PATERNOSTER ROW.

1876.

" In the days of those kingdoms, the God of Heaven will set up a kingdom that shall never be destroyed, and His kingdom shall not be delivered up to another people ; and it shall break in pieces and shall consume all these kingdoms, and itself shall stand for ever."

—Daniel.

DEAR CHILDREN,

You have seen an infant on its mother's knee turn to fix its eyes on a bright lamp or candle. If you go into a dark room you call for light. This desire for light is a gift of God. When He had created it He "saw that it was good." He kindled it from His own Being, whose light is from Everlasting. Those innumerable stars at which we gaze in wonder, He hung up in space on the morning of creation, and they will give light to the end of time.

Heaven was flooded with uncreated light, when Lucifer, through a sin of pride, sought to eclipse the glory of God by his own created light, and, from an angel of light, fell with the rest of the rebel angels into the blackness of darkness for ever. When men fell into

sin, and lost the light of God's grace, they
began to kindle fires to consume the victims
they had slain. This was done to draw down
the fire of His love upon their guilty souls.

From the earliest times smoke from these
fires rose up from altars of stone, in honour
of God and in thanksgiving, because in His
wrath He had remembered mercy. As time
went on a Greater Sacrifice approached,
longed for by God and man. My little
children, you know what that was. The
Holy Cross is the wood ; the victim, God
made man ; and the fire is the love of His
Sacred Heart. Faith and hope in this stu-
pendous sacrifice were kindled in the Garden
of Eden immediately after the Fall.

Holy patriarchs and prophets saw the
smoke of that sacrifice through the mist of
ages : the light from it was so brilliant that
it almost blinded them with joy before it had
been kindled : they were in the burning bush
of loving anticipation, and they speak of that
tremendous sacrifice as if it had been already

accomplished ; they seem to be looking back at, rather than forward to it. The prophet Isaias cries out, " The light of the moon shall be as the light of the sun, and the light of the sun shall be sevenfold ; in the day when the Lord shall bind up the wound of His people, and shall heal the stroke of their wound." . . . " The people that walked in darkness *have seen* a great light. For a child is born to us." The Immaculate Conception of the Blessed Virgin Mary is as the Sanctuary Lamp, through whose pure light the Orient from on high hath visited us. It shone through the drooping foliage of Paradise, when God said to the serpent,—" I will put enmities between thee and THE WOMAN . . . She shall crush thy head, and thou shalt lie in wait for her heel." Nothing defiled can touch our thrice holy God : therefore, He prepared an undefiled Tabernacle wherein to dwell, and shine on the darkness of this world, namely, the Body of His Virgin Mother. The Second Person of the ever - blessed

Trinity deigned to become Man in order to die for us, and the Immaculate Conception of His Mother reflects His uncreated Beauty and Divinity. The Sacrifice on Calvary was so tremendous that the smoke of it still goes up daily from the altars of the Christian Church, and will do so till the end of time ; in the words of the Catechism, "The MASS is *the unbloody sacrifice of the Body and Blood of Christ.*" The Lamb standing as it were slain. The prophet Malachi saw the glory of it, for he says, "The sacrifice of Juda and Jerusalem shall please the Lord as in the days of old." "From the rising of the sun even to the going down, my Name is great among the Gentiles, and in every place there is sacrifice, there is offered to my Name a clean oblation."

I have not space here to tell you all the types and figures of our Blessed Lord or of His Holy Church which are found in the Old Testament ; my wish is to point at the Lamp by whose light you may read them.

In the Book of Exodus it is written, the
Lord spoke to Moses, saying, "I have heard
the murmuring of the children of Israel ; . . .
say to them, . . . In the morning you shall
have your fill of bread, and you shall know
that I am the Lord your God. . . . And
when the children of Israel saw it, they said
one to another, *Manhu*, . . . what is this ? for
they knew not what it was. And Moses said
to them, this is the bread which the Lord
hath given you to eat. Fill a gomer of it,
and let it be kept unto generations to come
hereafter, that they may know the bread
wherewith I fed you . . . when you were
brought out of the land of Egypt."

It is within the tabernacle of the Holy
Catholic Church that the Heaven-sent bread
is stored for the strength and support of our
souls and bodies.

God made man is the Christian's *Manhu*,
and before Him the Sanctuary Lamp con-
tinually burns.

I write these words to you, dear children,

under the beautiful ruins of the church and
monastery of "The Blessed Mary and St.
Oswin," on the rugged cliffs of Northumber-
land.   Kings, Queens, Saints of every class in
life have knelt before its altar for centuries, to
contemplate and adore the Christian's Manhu,
the Lord our God.   Storm-tossed mariners
have hailed the twinkle of its altar lamp
through the foaming spray, and have called
upon their Sacramental Lord to command
the waters, and to say, "Peace, be still."
There are many such beautiful monasteries
and convents in England now ruined and
rifled, where holy men and women gave their
lives to God, and spent their time in praise,
in prayer, and in works of charity to their
neighbours, remembering the words of the
Divine Master whom they served, "Amen I
say to you, as long as you did it to one of
these my least brethren, you did it to me."

Besides the spiritual and corporal works
of mercy, they attained great perfection in
the fine arts—architecture, painting, music,

sculpture ; in the cloistered recesses of their religious houses they copied out by hand (for printing was unknown) the Holy Scriptures, of which the Church has always been the teacher, guided by the Third Person of the ever-Blessed Trinity, God the Holy Ghost.

Laid up in the colleges and museums of our land, these monuments of piety and zeal remain as a proof of the skill and industry of the religious Orders.

Dear children, you live in a land and in a time of *unbelief.* The enemy has sowed tares among the wheat. You will often hear the holy Church maligned. Remember then the words of her Blessed Lord, "If they have called the good-man of the house Beelzebub, how much more them of His household? therefore fear them not."

"You shall be hated by all men for my name's sake. . . . The disciple is not above his Master; it is enough for the disciple to be as his Master, and the servant as his Lord."

It is very necessary to bear these words of

our Blessed Lord in your mind, when the
devil and the world would seek to pour into
your young ears the deadly poison of hatred
against the Church which God has founded on
a rock, and against which He has said the gates
of hell shall not prevail.   In the words of the
Catechism, she cannot err in faith or morals,
for she is our infallible guide in both.   She
has four marks by which you may know her,
she is ONE—she is HOLY—she is CATHOLIC
—she is APOSTOLIC.   Her foundations are the
Prophets and Apostles, built on Christ the
Corner-stone; her Creeds are the pillars on
which she rests; her Lamp is a light to our
eyes and to our feet, and her reward the
eternal vision of God.

Soon after our Lord's Ascension, she suf-
fered persecution under the heathen Roman
Emperors.   "Sacrifice to our gods, or die!"
cried they.   "Let me die the death of the just,"
replied the Christian martyr as he looked at the
crucifix, "and let my last end be like to his."

Extinguished above ground, her Altar Lamp

was lighted in the dark recesses of the Cata-
combs, among the ashes of the dead. Those
persecutions passed away and others came
—yet she flourishes—her crown of thorns
stills bears its roses; persecution is to be her
portion, for she is Christ's Bride, and she
suffers with Him ; yet the odour of her
sanctity, emanating as it does from Him,
fills the whole world. Look abroad, dear
children of England ; in our day she is
raising her head from the effects of the dire
trial she had to endure during the reigns of
King Henry VIII. and Queen Elizabeth ; the
blood of martyrs again flowed.

Her ancient cathedrals and beautiful abbey
churches were grievously defaced, the axe of
the destroyer levelled her sculptured pillars
to the ground. The daily sacrifice of the
New Law was no longer offered in those
holy edifices. The sweet name of Mary was
profaned : the saints were no longer invoked ;
the words of the sweet singer of Israel were
hushed. The coarse voices of rough soldiers

were heard in the aisles, where the Psalms of holy David had been sung—" seven times a day." The dust of saints was scattered to the four winds.

The Lord's vineyard was rooted up. Still her faithful children clustered round her *Sanctuary Lamp* in some secluded church or room ; it shone more brightly in the darkness.

In whispered tones of love they sang her holy offices, the priest offered the Holy Sacrifice of the Mass, and in the words of the Psalmist exclaimed, while he wept, " Thy word is a light to my feet and a lantern to my path." Her garments, then so torn and disfigured, are now being repaired ; she is building up her waste places.

Her wounded sheep who fled in fear— called by the voice of the Great Shepherd— are returning to their beloved Fold, for there is one Fold and one Shepherd. Our own revered Cardinal Archbishop, with many other noble-hearted men and women of all conditions of life, have come and continue to come back out of darkness and doubt into her marvellous light; they are drawn by the light of her Sanctuary Lamp. Come, then, to the well of living water—our loving Saviour waits for *you*, as He did for the poor woman of Samaria; and though you have nothing wherein to draw, for the well is deep, say to Him with lively faith, " I know that the Messias cometh;" then He will embrace His humble child, and whisper those words of peace, " I am He who am speaking with thee."

In these days we are busied about many things, but one thing is necessary—Where is the House of our Faith?

On what foundation does it rest?

Take heed that it be not built on *sand*.

Glance over the pages of history. For 1800 years and more God's Church has withstood the tempests, and she has not fallen, for she is founded on a *Rock*—that Rock on which He built her. Prefigured in the Old Law, she is fulfilled in the New Law, and established for ever.

St. Peter received the Keys from his
Divine Master, and like a good steward of
the mysteries of God, he passed them on to
his successors, and there has not been want-
ing a man to sit on the Chair of Truth during
all that time. Taught and guided by the
Holy Ghost, the Spirit of truth, "whom the
world cannot receive—because it seeth Him
not nor knoweth Him"—the Holy Catholic
Church through the consecrated mouth of
Christ's Vicar has *infallibly spoken* the truth.
In the midst of trials, perplexities, wars, sins,
heresies, schisms, she has shone out—" fair
as the moon," lustrous, pure, and unsullied.
Her faithful children render implicit obedi-
ence to her chief Bishop, the successor of St.
Peter, but they likewise "render to Cæsar
the things that are Cæsar's." Her maxims
are those of her Lord. He taught us to love
God above all, and our neighbour as our-
selves—to take up our cross daily, and she
never fails to follow His example. He said
to His disciples before His Passion and

Death, " I have yet many things to say to you, but you cannot bear them now ; but when He, the Spirit of Truth, is come, He will teach you all Truth, and the things that *are to come* He will show you." The Holy Catholic Church, with such a Heavenly Guide— God Himself—*has never fallen into error.* But you may be told that she became corrupt, that reformation was needed. Look at this beautiful world in which we live. She turns on her axis by day and by night; does she shine less brightly in the firmament because men have disfigured her surface by their wickedness? Certainly not. She speeds on in her yearly orbit round the sun, whose light she reflects, and thus fulfils ner task till time is done. *Let light be made, and it was made.* Wilful heretics and schismatics the Church has cast out from her sacred Fold ; still ever ready to receive them back, she calls them to repentance and submission. She holds, and has held intact the Sacred Scriptures, and she is the living witness to their Truth ; it is through

B

her alone that we can receive the Gospels as
the Word of God.   Other truths the Holy
Ghost revealed to the Church which are
" not written."   She is Christ's Bride ; we are
her children, and we trust to her infallible
voice.

As we value our eternal salvation, men and
women, children of once Catholic England,
let us have recourse to the unction of the
Seven Sacraments, and to the other channels
of grace which the Church holds out : to her
alone belong the Creeds, and the Collects, and
the Epistles, and the Gospels whose echo you
hear on the first day of the week.   Her children fall low on the knee at those sweet words
of mercy, " Incarnatus est de Spiritu Sancto
ex Maria Virgine et *Homo Factus est ;* "
for her Lord is " Perfect God and perfect
man "—" not made, nor created, but begot-
ten."   The night is past, the day is at hand,
. . . . . . let us put on the armour of
light, and take oil in our lamps, that when
the Bridegroom cometh we may go out to

meet Him with joy—having passed through
the Church militant and suffering, may re-
joice for ever in the glories of the Church
triumphant.

So now, dear children, kneel often before the *Sanctuary Lamp*, and call on your
Lord, present in the Tabernacle, to give you
grace so to live that *your light* may shine
before men, that others seeing your good
works may glorify your Father who is in
heaven ; call to mind the lighted candle
which the priest of God's Church places in
the infant's hand in baptism : "Receive this
burning light, and keep thy baptism so as to
be without blame : observe the *commandments of God*, that when the Lord shall come
to the nuptials, thou mayest meet Him in
company of the saints in the heavenly court,
and have eternal life, and live for ever and
ever. Amen."

Pray, dear children, for holy souls departed,
and receive these few drops of oil from the

shrine of the Blessed Mary and St. Oswin; for though the noble priory is a ruin, and the stalls of the monks for three hundred years have been vacant,

The Sanctuary Lamp burns near.

C. M. B. S.,
TYNEMOUTH, *Feast of Corpus Christi,* 1876.

THE mission of Tynemouth was opened on the Feast of the Assumption, 1871. The chapel is a small temporary structure, wherein the Catholic soldiers assemble on Sundays during the Holy Sacrifice. A site has been secured, and efforts are being made with a view to erect a church worthy of this ancient abode of saints.

"Surge, Domine, in requiem tuam: tu et arca sanctificationes tuæ."

"Constituit eam super excelsam terram, ... ut sugeret mel de petra. Oleumque de saxo durissimo."

Deuteronomy xxxii. 13.

HAIL, holy Church of Rome,

  My true and only rest,

O lead me safely home

  To God for ever blest.

To thee the nations bow,

  For Catholic thou art ;

To souls pure, meek, and low

  Dost mysteries impart.

In Baptism's crystal wave
    Our sin-stained souls are washed,
One infant soul to save
    The Blood of Christ it cost.

Within yon lowly door
    Kind Penance long doth wait,
Now go and sin no more;
    Contrition's ne'er too late.

By Holy Spirit's light
    Through Confirmation's chrism,
We gain new strength to fight
    'Gainst heresy and schism.

Reflected clear is seen
In holy Marriage tie,
The Virgin-Mother-Queen,
A love that cannot die.

The virgins' crown is rare,
And decked with jewels bright ;
'Tis given those to wear
Whose robes are dazzling white.

O happy spouses ye
Who earth's false joys have fled,
And ever on the knee
Adore the Angels' Bread !

O wondrous, awful gift,
 In Ordination given,
That man his God may lift
 To plead with God in Heaven !

The " Star that never sets "
 Doth rise at daily Mass ;
'Tis God who pays our debts,
 But seen as in a glass.

The Eucharistic Bread,
 Our supersubstantial food,
By which our souls are fed,
 Christ's Body is and Blood.

In even one small crumb
  Divinity doth stop,
Incarnate God finds room
  In every single drop.

Raised high on Calvary's mount
  The Paschal Lamb lies slain,
His sacred Heart the fount,
  His Tears the healing rain.

Then haste to daily climb
  Up Calvary's ruddy steep ;
Until the end of time
  This fount springs pure and deep.

The Sun withdraws his light,
　　The veil is rent in twain,
God's Face is hid in night,
　　The heathen rage in vain.

The bonds are broke asunder,
　　Heaven's gates wide open fly,
That crash of fearful thunder
　　Proclaims God-Man doth die !

See Holy Church is born
　　When He her Lord doth die,
But speechless and forlorn
　　Still at His Feet doth lie.

Till opening wide her eyes
 God's Virgin-Mother sees—
" *Magnificat!* " she cries,
 Her widowed heart to ease.

St. Peter, where art thou? . ·
 Thy Master holds the key,
I hear thee whispering low, ·
 " O Lord, depart from me."

Yet Peter, lowly bend ;
 To thee the keys are given,
Nor earth nor hell can rend
 From thee that gift of Heaven.

Walk upon the water,
　　God's Ark is on the flood.
Meet Jesus, blessed Peter,
　　And seal thy faith in blood.

St. John denied Him not,
　　O happy Virgin blest,
T'was once thy envied lot
　　To lean upon His Breast,

And from the beating Heart
　　Draw secrets of His love,
In Patmos to impart
　　The glories stored above.

That Breast thou canst not reach,
   A sword hath pierced it through;
Thou standest near to teach
   What wretched *sin* will do.

The Blood-stained Feet await—
   Come, Magdalen, draw near,
Penance is not too late,
   True love doth cast out fear.

Come, Nicodemus meek,
   In this day's darkest night
Thy loving Saviour seek,
   For He will be thy light.

Arimathea's saint,
    Bring new white linen here,
No garb with earthly taint
    May shroud those Limbs so dear.

Now place Him in the tomb,
    " A watch " indeed is set,
Can there for man be room,
    When hosts of Heaven are met ?

Yes, men, saints, angels meet,
    His mother, too, is there ;
This is His Mercy-seat,
    Although He does not stir.

A Sabbath-day so " great "
  That God must rest thereon,
The seal it has been set
  Upon that ponderous stone.

The Eyes that looked abroad
  On fair Creation's dawn,
In death must be adored,
  Earth—sea, be still and mourn.

His Hands, His Feet, His Heart,
  Each worshipped be by us,
Divine each sacred part,
  Sanctus, Sanctus, Sanctus.

Whence come those glorious dyes
    That deck the Eastern sky?
Will earth's bright sun arise
    While Christ in death doth lie?

Bright Angel, take thy seat,
    That raiment dazzles me,
To guard thy God is meet,
    O honour high for thee.

That Angel low did speak,
    The women's eyes were dim—
" I know well whom ye seek,"
    All glory be to Him!

" Haste now to Galilee,
 He is not here" but there,
In truth Him ye shall see,
 Adore—and Him declare.

Peter and holy John,
 Make haste to run the race,
The folded linen con,
 But, Lord, show us Thy Face.

It shone on Thabor's hill,
 We could not bear It there;
Now risen, how It will
 Above the sun be fair!

But Thou hast turned aside
From this Thy garden-bed,
Show us where Thou dost hide,
Sweet Lily white and red.

His Mother blest, unstained
Would Jesu risen see,
" I to my beloved,
And my beloved to Me."

Redeemed before her birth
This Star precedes the sun,
Before Him shines on earth
But by His light alone.

" Ave Maria ! " Gabriel !

What voice repeats that sound ?

" Ave Jesu ! " earth and hell

With quaking fear rebound.

A second Eden this,

The tree of life is there,

No deadly serpents hiss ;—

" Take, eat—for it is fair."

Visible—Invisible,

Hail living Bread the Host ;

Risen—adorable,

Strive who can love Him most.

Magdalen "through the lattice"
  The gardener did spy.
" Mary," whispered Jesus.
  Hail, my God! " Rabboni!"

The hospitable two
  Who Him to Emmaus led,
The living Christ did view
  In broken crumbs of Bread.

The evening star doth shine,
  Dear stranger, with us stay ;
Our hearts within us burn,
  Ah, then, go not away.

O invitation sweet
  Unto the wearied—*rest.*
Yes, God would take His seat
  Within their glowing breast.

The merit of belief
  They happily attained,
While still their Lord and Chief
  Invisible remained.

O wavering Thomas, come,
  Look deep into His Hands ;
Read there the sceptic's doom,
  Then preach Him to all lands.

Believë and be baptized,
    Said Jesus when He rose ;
Believe not—be condemned :
    Man has free-will to choose.

.   .   .   .   .

Creator, Lord, Most High,
    My Judge and Saviour dear,
When the last day draws nigh,
    O unto me be near.

Reward the soul that brings
    Thy holy priest to me,
Before the death-knell rings
    My summons unto Thee.

For Extreme Unction's oil
  Doth strength and comfort give ;
Worn out with care and toil,
  Thy child would with Thee live

St. Michael, hover near,
  Hurl Satan far away,
O calm my mortal fear,
  Ora, ora, pro me.

Flash bright, my Rosary,
  Those charmed pebbles rare,
David's chain-armoury
  'Gainst proud Goliah's snare

Yes, aim with holy force
    The devil to disarm,
For *Ave* is the source
    That fills him with alarm.

Dread moment when I die,
    Sweet Mary, touch my hand,
And leave me not till I
    In Jesu's presence stand.

Then may my body lie
    'Midst faithful gone to rest,
No more again to die
    When glorified and blest.

The grave seems cold and dark,
Still drop, drop on, Church oil,
God's love—the living spark
That kindles Christian soil.

For holy souls now gone
Requiescant, daily say,
In pace, weeping groan
God's chastening arm to stay.

Indulgenced prayers still use
Through blessed Peter's key,
The debt of sin to loose,
Imprisoned souls to free.

Dear souls that loved us here,
　　Now flown to Jesu's Breast,
O whisper in our ear
　　The bliss of Heavenly rest.

List ! *watch*, for lo a cry,
　　Behold the Bridegroom near !
Nor go the oil to buy,
　　Meet Him with holy fear.

But work while it is day,
　　Fear not the grave's dark night,
Christ Jesus is our stay,
　　And He will be our light.

The lamp of holy Church
  Undimmed will ever glow,
For truth then in her search,
  Her oil doth overflow.

Hell's gates shall ne'er prevail
  This Church to overthrow,
Though wicked men will rail,
  Yet God their pride lays low.

Persecuted by man,
  Thy crown—of thorns is now ;
Triumphant soon thou'lt reign,
  With jewels on thy brow.

The Holy Scriptures lie
  Deep set within thy wall,
Guarded by God's clear Eye,
  Heresy to appal.

Still sculptured clear in stone
  The Ten Commandments stand,
O keep them every one
  Their prize—the promised land.

O lamp of holy Church,
  We know where Jesus lives,
Guide others there to search,
  And find the *Bread He gives.*

Still shine upon those doors,
    Fast-closed doors, where He
The Bread of Angels stores,
    Our precious food to be.

Bright emblem of the Star
    That stood o'er Bethlehem's shed,
Wise men will still be there,
    By Holy Spirit led.

.   .   .   .   .

O when the stone rolls back,
    And buried saints arise,
No work nor prayer they'll lack
    When Christ comes in the skies.

That second Easter morn
  Will spring to life and light,
For evermore to dawn,
  No more to sink in night.

Earth's sun shall run his course,
  The moon her light resign;
But LIGHT OF LIGHTS, their source,
  Will everlasting shine.

Blest, blissful Tri-une Light,
  The saints reflect but Thee;
Keep Thou the Church oil bright,
  Lumen de Lumine!

God of God one alone,

    Persons Three—equal each,

Deum de Deo—one

    Still deign meek babes to teach.

With Thee there is no night,

    Thrice Blessed Three in One;

Hail, UNCREATED LIGHT,

    For Thou art God alone!

Holp Souls departed

with

Oil in your lamps,

May Eternal Light enlighten you.

THE city hath no need of the sun nor of the moon to shine in it. For the glory of God hath enlightened it, and the Lamb is the lamp thereof. And the nations shall walk in the light of it : and the kings of the earth shall bring their glory and honour into it. And the gates thereof shall not be shut by day : for there shall be no night there.—*Apocalypse.*

Blessed be God.
Blessed be His Holy name.
Blessed be Jesus Christ, true God and true man.
Blessed be the name of Jesus.
Blessed be Jesus in the most Holy Sacrament of the Altar.
Blessed be the great Mother of God, Mary most holy.
Blessed be her Holy and Immaculate Conception.
Blessed be the name of Mary, Virgin and Mother.
Blessed be God in His Angels and in His Saints.

www.ingramcontent.com/pod-product-compliance
Lightning Source LLC
Chambersburg PA
CBHW032121080426
42733CB00008B/1003